SRA
Reading Mastery
Signature Edition

Language Assessment Handbook

Grade 1

Siegfried Engelmann
Jerry Silbert

McGraw Hill SRA

Columbus, OH

This handbook is based on items written by
Siegfried Engelmann, Jean Osborn,
and Karen Lou Seitz Davis.

SRAonline.com

 SRA

Send all inquiries to this address:
SRA/McGraw-Hill
8787 Orion Place
Columbus, OH 43240

ISBN: 978-0-07-623484-4
MHID: 0-07-623484-3

5 6 7 8 9 QDB 13 12 11

The McGraw-Hill Companies

■■■■■■■■■ Contents ■■■■■■■■■

LANGUAGE ASSESSMENT HANDBOOK

Introduction

This Assessment Handbook includes thirteen program assessments to be given at ten (or twenty) lesson intervals, beginning when the children complete lesson 10 and ending when they complete lesson 130 of the **Reading Mastery** Signature Edition Grade 1 Language program. These assessments will provide you with information that will help you monitor the progress of the children as they move through the program. The assessments will also help you identify any children who need extra help.

Directions for giving and scoring the assessments are on pages 2–3. The assessments, in the form of reproducible Individual Score Sheets, are on pages 7–31. Group Summary Sheets to record the performance of each student in the group begin on page 32.

The assessments are criterion-referenced, which means that they evaluate each child's achievement within the program. Each of the thirteen assessments measures student understanding of a specific set of concepts from the Grade 1 Language program.

The assessments were written to be available at ten-lesson intervals so that you can have access to an appropriate assessment for each of your groups, no matter where they are in the program. For example, you give Assessment 1 after the children have completed lesson 10. Because you want to closely monitor the progress of this group, you decided that you will give Assessment 2 when the group completes lesson 20. You predict that you need to give the children in this group the assessment for each ten-lesson block.

Here is another example. You decide to give Assessment 1 to a group of children who are doing well in the program. You give this assessment the day after the group has completed lesson 10. The children do very well, and you decide that you probably won't need to assess them again until they complete lesson 30. You will give them Assessment 3 at that time and continue at twenty-lesson intervals (skipping even-numbered assessments) during the remainder of the program.

You may be part of a schoolwide assessment plan that has determined that students will be assessed in each subject area on a regular schedule, for example, at twenty-lesson intervals. In this case you could present Assessment 2 following lesson 20, continuing at twenty-lesson intervals in this way during the remainder of the program (skipping odd-numbered assessments).

Administering and Scoring Assessments

Directions for Giving the Assessments

When Administer an assessment at the end of each ten- or twenty-lesson block. A program Assessment is to be given after the students complete a specified program lesson. For example, Assessment 1 is given when the children complete lesson 10; Assessment 6 when they complete lesson 60.

Time Requirements The first eight assessments are all oral. Most children require about five minutes to complete each of the assessments. Remember that each item in each assessment is to be presented individually and that the children must be given adequate time to respond. Beginning with Assessment 9, there is a group writing assessment as well as individual testing for each child. The group writing assessments should take about ten minutes.

Materials To give an assessment, you will need this handbook, an Individual Score Sheet for each student, and a pencil. For each assessment, there is an Individual Score Sheet that has the questions for the assessment and a space for recording if the student responded correctly or incorrectly to each question or task. You will need to make a copy of the score sheet form for each student.

For Assessments 6 and 7, you will use maps 6D and 7E, which appear in this handbook. For Assessments 9–13, you will need to make a copy of the Part A Writing Assessment for each student.

There is a Group Summary Score Sheet for each assessment. This group summary has spaces for each part of the assessment and for each student. You record how many parts each student passed. The Group Summary Sheet shows which parts the group is having difficulty with. (See pages 32–38.)

The following text styles are used in each assessment:

- Th s text, in blue or black, indicates what you say.

- (Text in parentheses indicates what you do or what the child does.)

- *Italics indicate the child's spoken responses.*

Where Choose a fairly quiet place in your classroom. It is important that you are able to hear the child's responses.

How Present each item exactly as written, and listen carefully to the child's response. Move from item to item at a good pace.

Directions for Scoring Assessments

The Individual Score Sheets Each Individual Score Sheet lists an item number for each scorable response. Record the child's responses on the Individual Score Sheet by circling + or -.

Evaluating Student Responses Present each item as written. Give the child time to respond to your instructions and questions. The correct responses are specified in the assessment materials. If a child gives a response that is not specified but is a reasonable response, accept the alternative response as correct. If the child does not respond after a ten-second interval, mark the item as incorrect and move on to the next item.

Statement Production Items Statement production items require the student to say a specified statement in response to the direction, "Say the statement." To receive credit, a child must produce the full statement as written. Do not give credit for a response that omits words or substitutes other words for those in the statement.

Sentence-Writing Items Sentence-writing items begin on Assessment 9 and appear on each assessment through Assessment 13. You will need to reproduce worksheets for each student for the sentence-writing part of the test.

Test Remedies

Test remedies are indicated for students who miss assessment items. It is possible to use formulas for administering test remedies (if $\frac{1}{4}$ of the students miss an item, present the remedy); however, the goal of the remedies would be to fix up each student's understanding. Generally, students who make more than one mistake on any part of the test should receive a remedy for that part.

The test remedies that follow (pages 4–6) specify exercises that should be repeated for the missed parts of the tests. Although the workbook is copyrighted and may not normally be reproduced, you may reproduce the part of the workbook needed for test remedies. After firming students on test remedies, repeat the test or the part of the test the student failed.

Test Remedies: Assessments 1–5

If ¼ or more of the students do not pass a part, present the remedy exercises for the part.

Test	Test Part Failed	To Remedy, Present:					
		Lesson	Exercise	Lesson	Exercise	Lesson	Exercise
Assessment 1 Lesson 10	A Calendar Facts	7	4	8	3		
	B Where—When	5	3	6	4	7	2
	C Classification	6	1	8	5	9	2
	D Same—Different	8	4	9	6	10	5
	E Actions	5	1	8	1	9	1
Assessment 2 Lesson 20	A Opposites	17	7	18	3	20	4
	B Sequence	14	3	15	6	16	2
	C True—False	14	5	15	2	16	6
	D Actions	12	1	13	1	14	1
	E Same—Different	12	6	13	5	14	4
Assessment 3 Lesson 30	A Only	22	5	23	2	25	2
	B Calendar	23	7				
	C Classification	23	5	24	3	25	5
	D Opposites	22	7	24	4	25	4
	E Who—Where—When—What	24	5	25	3	28	2
Assessment 4 Lesson 40	A Who—How—Why	34	4	37	6	40	3
	B From—To			37	2		
	C Questioning Skills	32	6	33	3	38	6
	D Calendar	34	3				
	E Classification	33	4	34	1	35	4
Assessment 5 Lesson 50	A Who—What—When—Where—Why	46	5	47	5	48	9
	B Classification	42	3	44	2	46	3
	C Verb Tense	43	5	46	1	48	3
	D From—To	42	5			48	2
	E Description	47	4	48	8	49	4

Test Remedies: Assessments 6–9

If ¹/₄ or more of the students do not pass a part, present the remedy exercises for the part.

Test	Test Part Failed	To Remedy, Present:					
		Lesson	Exercise	Lesson	Exercise	Lesson	Exercise
Assessment 6 Lesson 60	A Classification	52	2	53	5	55	2
	B True—False	53	4	56	4	57	2
	C Description	51	2	52	3	57	1
	D Map Reading	50	8	52	6	53	7
	E Opposites	55	4	56	2	57	3
Assessment 7 Lesson 70	A Classification	64	1	65	4		
	B Statements	63	2	65	2	67	4
	C Analogies	65	6	66	2	67	5
	D Opposites	62	4	66	3	67	1
	E Map Reading	62	8	65	9		
Assessment 8 Lesson 80	A Synonyms	77	2	78	4	79	4
	B True—False	74	2	75	3	76	1
	C Who—What—When—Where—Why	72	5	74	6	76	2
	D Analogies	76	5	77	4	78	3
	E Can Do	72	6	73	4	74	5
Assessment 9 Lesson 90	A Sentence Writing	83	8	84	5		
	B Calendar Facts	83	7	84	1	89	4
	C Analogies	81	2	82	1	86	1
	D Who—What—When—Where—Why	85	5	85	7	86	8
	E Map Reading	82	3	83	4	85	5
	F Synonyms	81	6	83	5	84	4

Test Remedies: Assessments 10–13

If ¼ or more of the students do not pass a part, present the remedy exercises for the part.

Test	Test Part Failed	To Remedy, Present:					
		Lesson	Exercise	Lesson	Exercise	Lesson	Exercise
Assessment 10 Lesson 100	A Sentence Writing	92	6	93	6		
	B Analogies	93	1	94	4	95	1
	C Who—What—When—Where—Why	92	1	94	5	95	4
	D Synonyms/Opposites	96	3	97	4	98	1
	E Statements	95	3	96	4	98	2
	F Description	92	4	93	3	94	1
Assessment 11 Lesson 110	A Sentence Writing	104	6	105	6		
	B Opposites	101	2	102	2	104	3
	C Synonyms/Opposites	106	4	107	5		
	D Analogies	103	1	104	2	105	1
	E Classification	103	3	104	5	105	3
	F Verb Tense	102	5	109	3	110	3
Assessment 12 Lesson 120	A Sentence Writing	114	7				
	B Description	112	3	114	3	116	3
	C Statements	114	4	118	2		
	D Synonyms	114	1	115	3	116	4
	E Verb Tense	110	3	112	4	119	2
	F If—Then	116	1	117	1	118	5
Assessment 13 Lesson 130	A Sentence Writing	122	6	124	5		
	B Verb Tense	122	2	123	1	124	2
	C Contractions	122	5	124	1	127	1
	D Absurdity	125	4	127	5	128	4
	E Opposites	121	3	122	4	123	5
	F Who—What—When—Where—Why	120	1	127	4		

Individual Score Sheet—Assessment 1

Student Name _____ Date _____

(Present each item. Circle + or − for each response. Responses must be verbatim unless enclosed in parentheses.)

A. Calendar Facts

1.	How many days are in a week?	7.	+	−
2.	Say the seven days of the week.	Sunday, Monday. Tuesday, Wednesday, Thursday, Friday, Saturday.	+	−
3.	How many months are in a year?	12.	+	−
4.	Name the months of the year.	January, February, March, April, May, June, July, August, September, October, November, December.	+	−
5.	How many seasons are in a year?	4.	+	−
6.	Say the seasons of the year.	Winter, spring, summer, fall.	+	−

Pass = 5/6 or more correct (Not pass = more than 1 error)   P   NP

B. Where—When

•	I'll say statements. Some will tell when. Some will tell where. Some will tell neither.			
1.	We rode our bikes very fast. Tell me when, where, or neither.	Neither.	+	−
2.	We rode our bikes on a dirt road. Tell me when, where, or neither.	Where.	+	−
3.	Where did we ride our bikes?	On a dirt road.	+	−
4.	We road our bikes yesterday. Tell me when, where, or neither.	When.	+	−
5.	When did we ride our bikes?	Yesterday.	+	−

Pass = 4/5 or more correct (Not pass = more than 1 error)   P   NP

C. Classification

•	I'm going to name some objects. Tell me a class these objects are in.			
1.	Truck, car, train, motorcycle, boat. What class?	Vehicle.	+	−
2.	Hammer, shovel, pliers, saw, hoe. What class?	Tools.	+	−
3.	Cake, rice, beans, milk, bread. What class?	Food.	+	−
4.	Chair, sofa, bed, lamp, rug, cabinet. What class?	Furniture.	+	−
5.	Fire station, house, grocery store, school. What class?	Building	+	−

Pass = 4/5 or more correct (Not pass = more than 1 error)   P   NP

D. Same—Different

•	You're going to tell how things are the same and how they are different.			
1.	Tell me 1 way that a paper bag and a suitcase are the same.	(Accept reasonable answer.)	+	−
2.	Tell me 1 way that a paper bag and a suitcase are different.	(Accept reasonable answer.)	+	−
3.	Tell me 1 way that a shirt and a coat are the same.	(Accept reasonable answer.)	+	−
4.	Tell me 1 way that a shirt and a coat are different.	(Accept reasonable answer.)	+	−

Pass = 4/4 correct (Not pass = 1 or more errors)   P   NP

E. Actions

1.	Listen. I'm going to clap my hands or shake my foot. What am I going to do?	(Clap your hands or shake your foot.)	+	−
2.	I'm going to clap my hands or shake my foot. Am I going to shake my foot?	Maybe.	+	−
3.	Am I going to stand up?	No.	+	−
4.	Am I going to clap my hands?	Maybe.	+	−
•	Here I go. (Shake your foot.)			
5.	Did I clap my hands?	No.	+	−
6.	Did I shake my foot?	Yes.	+	−

Pass = 5/6 or more correct (Not pass = more than 1 error)   P   NP

Test Remedies   7

Individual Score Sheet—Assessment 2

Student Name _____ Date _____

(Present each item. Circle + or – for each response. Responses must be verbatim unless enclosed in parentheses.)

A. Opposites

•	I'll say words. You tell me the opposite.			
1.	What's the opposite of **empty?**	Full		
2.	**Full** is the opposite of what?	Empty.	+	–
3.	Say the whole thing about full.	Full is the opposite of empty.	+	–
4.	What's the opposite of **old?**	Young (or New).	+	–
5.	Say the whole thing about young.	Young (or New) is the opposite of old.	+	–
6.	What's the opposite of **tall?**	Short.	+	–
7.	Say the whole thing about short.	Short is the opposite of tall (or long).	+	–
Pass = 6/7 or more correct (Not pass = more than 1 error)			P	NP

B. Sequence

•	I'll tell you four things that happened. Listen.			
•	First, Sarah picked up her toothbrush and toothpaste. Next, she opened the toothpaste. Next, she put toothpaste on her toothbrush. Last, she brushed her teeth.			
•	Listen again. (Repeat story.)			
1.	Tell me the four things. What happened first?	(Idea: Sarah picked up her toothbrush and toothpaste.)	+	–
2.	What happened next?	(Idea: She opened the toothpaste.)	+	–
3.	What happened next?	(Idea: She put toothpaste on her toothbrush.)	+	–
4.	What happened last?	(Idea: She brushed her teeth.)	+	–
5.	I'll say the four things, but I'm going to make mistakes. As soon as you hear a mistake, say **stop,** then tell me the right thing that happened. Listen. First, Sarah picked up her toothbrush and toothpaste. Next, she brushed her teeth.	(Child says stop.)	+	–
6.	What happened after Sarah picked up her toothbrush and toothpaste?	She opened the toothpaste.	+	–
Pass = 5/6 or more correct (Not pass = more than 1 error)			P	NP

C. True—False

•	I'm going to make statements about a house. Listen. Say **true** if I make a statement that is right. Say **false** if I make a statement that is not right.			
1.	A house can fly. Is that true or false?	False.	+	–
2.	A house has walls. Is that true or false?	True.	+	–
3.	A house has a door. Is that true or false?	True.	+	–
4.	A house has wings. Is that true or false?	False.	+	–
5.	A house can take you places. Is that true or false?	False.	+	–
6.	A house has a roof. Is that true or false?	True.	+	–
Pass = 5/6 or more correct (Not pass = more than 1 error)			P	NP

D. Actions

1.	I'm going to jump or stamp my foot or sit down. What am I going to do?	Jump or stamp your foot or sit down.	+	–
2.	I'm going to jump or stamp my foot or sit down. Am I going to jump?	Maybe.	+	–
3.	Am I going to sit down?	Maybe.	+	–
4.	Am I going to run?	No.	+	–
5.	Am I going to stamp my foot?	Maybe.	+	–
6.	Here I go. (Stamp your foot.) Did I sit down?	No.	+	–
7.	Did I stamp my foot?	Yes.	+	–
8.	What did I do?	Stamp(ed) your foot.	+	–
9.	Say the whole thing.	You stamped your foot.	+	–
Pass = 8/9 or more correct (Not pass = more than 1 error)			P	NP

E. Same—Different

•	We're going to talk about how things are the same and how they are different.			
1.	A chalkboard and paper—Tell me one way they are the same.	(Accept reasonable answer.)	+	–
2.	A chalkboard and paper—See if you can name one way they are different.	(Accept reasonable answer.)	+	–
3.	Here's another one. Scissors and a knife—See if you can name one way they are the same.	(Accept reasonable answer.)	+	–
4.	Scissors and a knife—See if you can name one way they are different.	(Accept reasonable answer.)	+	–
Pass = 4/4 correct (Not pass = 1 or more errors)			P	NP

Individual Score Sheet—Assessment 3

Student Name _____ Date _____

Materials for Part B: Calendar

(Present each item. Circle + or – for each response. Responses must be verbatim unless enclosed in parentheses.)

A. Only

•	I'm going to make statements. Each statement is going to be true of only a boat or only a motorcycle or both a boat and a motorcycle.			
1.	It goes on the highway. Tell me what that statement is true of.	*Only a motorcycle.*	+	–
2.	It goes in the water. Tell me what that statement is true of.	*Only a boat.*	+	–
3.	It is a vehicle. Tell me what that statement is true of.	*(Both a boat and a motorcycle.)*	+	–
4.	Make up a statement that is true of **only** a boat.	*(Accept reasonable answer.)*	+	–
5.	Make up a statement that is true of **both** a boat and a motorcycle.	*(Accept reasonable answer.)*	+	–

Pass = 4.5 or more correct (Not pass = more than 1 error)   P   NP

B. Calendar

•	(Present calendar.) First, you'll tell me about the days of the week. Then you'll tell me about the dates. Today is ____ day. Today's date is _____.			
1.	Tell me the day of the week it was yesterday.	*(Correct day.)*	+	–
2.	Tell me the day of the week it will be tomorrow.	*(Correct day.)*	+	–
3.	Now the dates. Tell me yesterday's date.	*(Correct date.)*	+	–
4.	Tell me tomorrow's date.	*(Correct date.)*	+	–

Pass = 4/4 correct (Not pass = 1 or more errors)   P   NP

C. Classification

•	Remember the rule about bigger classes. The bigger class has more kinds of things in it. I'll say classes. You tell me which class is the biggest.			
1.	Farm animals, animals, chickens—Which of those classes is the biggest?	*Animals.*	+	–
2.	Men, women, people—Which of those classes is the biggest?	*People.*	+	–
3.	Plants, living things, grass—Which of those classes is the biggest?	*Living things.*	+	–
4.	Wild animals, bears, animals—Which of those classes is the biggest?	*Animals.*	+	–

Pass = 4/4 correct (Not pass = 1 or more errors)   P   NP

D. Opposites

•	Tell me about opposites.			
1.	I'm thinking of a stream that is the opposite of quiet. So what do you know about it?	*It's noisy.*	+	–
2.	I'm thinking of a road that is the opposite of narrow. So what do you know about it?	*It's wide.*	+	–
3.	I'm thinking of children who are the opposite of noisy. So what do you know about them?	*They're quiet.*	+	–
4.	I'm thinking of a tiger that is the opposite of awake. So what do you know about it?	*It's asleep.*	+	–

Pass = 4/4 correct (Not pass = 1 or more errors)   P   NP

E. Who—Where—When—What

•	I'm going to say a sentence that answers the questions about who, where, when, and what. You'll answer the questions. Listen. Last night, two birds flew into the nest. Listen again. Last night, two birds flew into the nest.			
1.	Your turn. Say the sentence.	*Last night, two birds flew into the nest.*	+	–
2.	Who flew into the nest?	*Two birds.*	+	–
3.	What did the birds do?	*Flew into the nest.*	+	–
4.	When did the birds do that?	*Last night.*	+	–
5.	Where did the birds go?	*Into the nest.*	+	–

Pass = 4/5 or more correct (Not pass = more than 1 error)   P   NP

Language Assessment Handbook   **9**

Individual Score Sheet—Assessment 4

Student Name _____ Date _____

Materials: Piece of paper (Part B); Calendar (Part D)

(Present each item. Circle + or – for each response. Responses must be verbatim unless enclosed in parentheses.)

A. Who—How—Why

1.	The boys slept soundly because they had done a lot of work. Listen again. The boys slept soundly because they had done a lot of work. Say the sentence.	*The boys slept soundly because they had done a lot of work.*	+	–
2.	How did the boys sleep?	*Soundly.*	+	–
3.	Who slept soundly?	*The boys.*	+	–
4.	Why did they sleep soundly?	*Because they had done a lot of work.*	+	–
	Pass = 4/4 correct (Not pass = 1 or more errors)		P	NP

B. From—To

•	(Draw a small circle on a piece of paper.) Tell me if I move my finger **from** the circle.			
1.	(Place your finger to the left of the circle.) Watch. (Move it toward the circle.) Did I move from the circle?	*No.*	+	–
2.	(Place your finger inside the circle.) Watch. (Move it straight up from the circle.) Did I move from the circle?	*Yes.*	+	–
3.	(Place your finger inside the circle.) Watch. (Move it from the circle to the left.) Did I move from the circle?	*Yes.*	+	–
4.	(Place your finger above the circle.) Watch. (Move it straight down to the circle.) Did I move from the circle?	*No.*	+	–
	Pass = 4/4 correct (Not pass = 1 or more errors)		P	NP

C. Questioning Skills

•	I'm thinking about something. It's either a glove, a hammer, a cup, or a pot. You'll ask questions to find out which object I'm thinking of.			
1.	Ask a question about the parts it has.	*(Idea: What parts does it have? or other acceptable question.)*	+	–
•	Here's the answer. It has a handle and a bowl.			
2.	Ask the question about what you use it for.	*(What do you use it for?)*	+	–
•	Here's the answer. You use it to drink from.			
3.	Ask the question about where you can find it.	*(Where can you find it?)*	+	–
•	Here's the answer. You could find it in a kitchen.			
4.	What object was I thinking of: a suitcase, a hammer, a cup, or a pot?	*A cup.*	+	–
5.	How did you know I wasn't thinking of a pot?	*(Idea: You don't drink from it.)*	+	–
	Pass = 4/5 or more correct (Not pass = more than 1 error)		P	NP

D. Calendar

•	(Present calendar.) We're going to talk about today, tomorrow, and one week from today. Today is ____day. Today's date is _____.			
1.	Tell me the day of the week it will be tomorrow.	(Correct day.)	+	–
2.	Tell me the day of the week it will be one week from today.	(Correct day.)	+	–
3.	Now the dates. Tell me yesterday's date.	(Correct day.)	+	–
4.	Say the date that it is one week from today.	(Correct day.)	+	–
	Pass = 4/4 correct (Not pass = 1 or more errors)		P	NP

E. Classification

	We're going to talk about classes.			
1.	If we took all potatoes from the class of food, would there be any kinds of food left?	*Yes.*	+	–
2.	Name two kinds of food that would be left.	(Accept reasonable answers.)	+	–
3.	The class of potatoes is made up of many kinds of potatoes. Name two kinds of potatoes in the class of potatoes.	(Accept reasonable answer such as mashed potatoes and baked potatoes or red potatoes and sweet potatoes.)	+	–
4.	Which class is bigger, the class of potatoes or the class of food?	*The class of food.*	+	–
5.	Which class is bigger, the class of potatoes or the class of mashed potatoes?	*The class of potatoes.*	+	–
	Pass = 4/5 or more correct (Not pass = more than 1 error)		P	NP

Individual Score Sheet—Assessment 5

Student Name _____ Date _____

(Present each item. Circle + or – for each response. Responses must be verbatim unless enclosed in parentheses.)

A. Who—What—When—Where—Why

•	Listen to this story.			
•	The man woke up early in the morning. He was very sleepy, so he drank some coffee. After he drank the coffee, he went to work in his garage.			
•	Listen again. (Repeat story.)			
1.	Tell who woke up.	*The man.*	+	–
2.	Tell when the man woke up.	*(Early in the) morning.*	+	–
3.	Tell why the man drank some coffee.	*(Because he was very sleepy.)*	+	–
4.	Tell what the man did after he drank the coffee.	*(Went to work.)*	+	–
5.	Tell where the man went to work.	*In his garage.*	+	–

Pass = 4/5 or more correct   (Not pass = more than 1 error)   P   NP

B. Classification

1.	Tell me which class has the most kinds of things in it— oak trees, trees, plants, or living things.	*Living things.*	+	–
2.	You're going to name some classes an oak tree is in. (Make a circle with your hands.) What's the smallest class for an oak tree?	*Oak trees.*	+	–
3.	(Make a wider circle.) What's the next bigger class?	*Trees.*	+	–
4.	(Make a still wider circle.) What's a really big class?	*Plants. (If child says living things, ask 5A, not 5.)*	+	–
5.	(Make an even wider circle.) What's a really big class?	*Living things.*	+	–
5.A	(If child responded *living things* to item 4:) What class is bigger than trees and smaller than living things?	*Plants.*	(5 or 5A)	

Pass = 4/5 or more correct   (Not pass = more than 1 error)   P   NP

C. Verb Tense

•	Today the bugs **are** in the garden. Yesterday the bugs **were** in the garden. Tomorrow the bugs **will be** in the garden.			
1.	Make the statement about the bugs today.	*Today the bugs are in the garden.*	+	–
2.	Make the statement about the bugs yesterday.	*Yesterday the bugs were in the garden.*	+	–
3.	Make the statement about the bugs tomorrow.	*Tomorrow the bugs will be in the garden.*	+	–

Pass = 3/3 correct   (Not pass = 1 or more errors)   P   NP

D. From—To

•	I'm going to move my finger from something to something else. See if you can tell me how my finger moves.			
1.	My turn. (Place your finger on your ear.) Watch. (Move it to your nose.) I did it. Where did my finger move from?	*(Idea: Your ear.)*	+	–
2.	Where did my finger move to?	*(Your nose.)*	+	–
3.	How did I move my finger?	*(From your ear to your nose.)*	+	–
4.	Say the whole thing about how I moved my finger.	*(You moved your finger from your ear to your nose.)*	+	–

Pass = 4/4 correct   (Not pass = 1 or more errors)   P   NP

E. Description

1.	I'm thinking of an object. See if you can figure out what object I'm thinking of. I'll tell you something about the object. It's an animal. What do you know about the object?	*It's an animal.*	+	–
2.	Could I be thinking of a wagon?	*No.*	+	–
3.	Could I be thinking of a cow?	*Yes.*	+	–
•	The object I'm thinking of is an animal, **and** you find it in the jungle.			
4.	Could I be thinking of an elephant?	*Yes.*	+	–
5.	Could I be thinking of a polar bear?	*No.*	+	–
6.	Why not?	*You do not find it in a jungle.*	+	–
7.	The object I'm thinking of is an animal, **and** you find it in the jungle, **and** it has stripes. What is the animal I am thinking of?	*A tiger.*	+	–

Pass = 6/7 or more correct   (Not pass = more than 1 error)   P   NP

Language Assessment Handbook

Individual Score Sheet—Assessment 6

Student Name _____ Date _____

Materials for Part D: Assessment 6 map (page 13)

(Present each item. Circle + or – for each response. Responses must be verbatim unless enclosed in parentheses.)

A. Classification

•	We can put a rocking chair into three different classes. See how many classes you can name, starting with the smallest class.			
1.	What's the smallest class for a rocking chair?	Rocking chair(s).	+	–
2.	What's the next bigger class?	Chair(s).	+	–
3.	What's the next bigger class?	Furniture.	+	–
4.	What is one kind of object you would find in all those classes?	A rocking chair.	+	–
5.	Would you find a table in all those classes?	No.	+	–
6.	Name the class you would find a table in.	Furniture.	+	–
	Pass = 5/6 or more correct (Not pass = more than 1 error)		P	NP

B. True—False

•	I'm going to say statements. Some of these statements are true and some are false.			
1.	You wear shoes on your hands. True or false?	False.	+	–
2.	A bottle is a plant. True or false?	False.	+	–
3.	Cats have claws. True or false?	True.	+	–
4.	A boat has wheels. True or false?	False.	+	–
5.	Make up a statement about a boat that is true.	(Accept reasonable answer.)	+	–
6.	Now make up a statement about a boat that is false.	(Accept reasonable answer.)	+	–
	Pass = 5/6 or more correct (Not pass = more than 1 error)		P	NP

C. Description

•	You're going to figure out what object I'm thinking of.			
1.	I'm thinking of a vehicle that has wheels. Name 2 vehicles I could be thinking of.	(Accept reasonable answers.)	+	–
2.	I'm thinking of a vehicle with wheels that carries a lot of people. Could I be thinking of a boat?	No.	+	–
3.	How do you know?	(It's not a vehicle with wheels.)	+	–
4.	Could I be thinking of a motorcycle?	No.	+	–
5.	How do you know?	(It doesn't carry a lot of people.)	+	–
6.	Could I be thinking of a train?	Yes.	+	–
7.	How do you know?	(It's a vehicle with wheels that carries a lot of people.)	+	–
8.	The vehicle I'm thinking of runs on tracks. Could I be thinking of a train?	Yes.	+	–
	Pass = 7/8 or more correct (Not pass = more than 1 error)		P	NP

D. Map Reading
Material: Map, page 13 (or Workbook, Lesson 56, Side 2)

•	You are going to tell me the direction the arrows with a letter are pointing. (Display Part D Map.)			
1.	Touch **A.** Which direction is that arrow pointing?	East.	+	–
2.	Touch **B.** Which direction is that arrow pointing?	West.	+	–
3.	Touch **C.** Which direction is that arrow pointing?	South.	+	–
4.	Touch **D.** Which direction is that arrow pointing?	North.	+	–
	Pass = 4/4 correct (Not pass = 1 or more errors)		P	NP

E. Opposites

•	You're going to make up statements that have the opposite word.			
•	The street was dangerous. Say that statement.	The street was dangerous.		
1.	Now say a statement that tells the opposite about the street.	(The street was safe.)	+	–
•	The table top was smooth. Say that statement.	The table top was smooth.		
2.	Now say a statement that tells the opposite about the table top.	(The table top was rough.)	+	–
•	The car was shiny. Say that statement.	The car was shiny.		
3.	Now say a statement that tells the opposite about the car.	(The car was dull.)	+	–
	Pass = 3/3 correct (Not pass = 1 or more errors)		P	NP

North

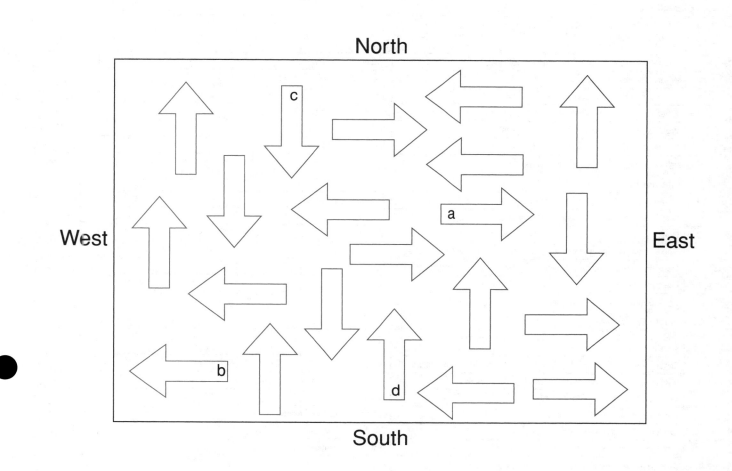

West

East

South

Individual Score Sheet—Assessment 7

Student Name _____ Date _____

Materials for Part E: Assessment 7 map (page 15)

(Present each item. Circle + or – for each response. Responses must be verbatim unless enclosed in parentheses.)

A. Classification

•	We're going to talk about mashed potatoes. We can put mashed potatoes into three different classes. You'll name three classes, starting with the smallest class.			
1.	What's the smallest class for mashed potatoes?	*Mashed potatoes.*	+	–
2.	What's the next bigger class?	*(Idea: Potatoes or other reasonable class.)*	+	–
3.	What's the biggest class?	*(Idea: Food.)*	+	–
4.	What is one kind of object you would find in all those classes?	*Mashed potatoes.*	+	–
5.	Would you find a carrot in all those classes?	*No.*	+	–
6.	Which of these classes would you find a carrot in?	*Food.*	+	–
Pass = 5/6 or more correct (Not pass = more than 1 error)			P	NP

B. Statements

1.	Listen to this statement. They are flying kites. Say that statement.	*They are flying kites.*	+	–
2.	Does that statement tell you if they are girls?	*No.*	+	–
3.	Does that statement tell you if they are wearing coats?	*No.*	+	–
4.	Does that statement tell you what they are doing now?	*Yes.*	+	–
5.	Does that statement tell you what they will be doing tomorrow?	*No.*	+	–
6.	Does that statement tell you if the kites are big?	*No.*	+	–
Pass = 5/6 or more correct (Not pass = more than 1 error)			P	NP

C. Analogies

•	You are going to make up sentences that are like the sentence I start with.			
1.	Listen. A newspaper is made of some material. What material?	*Paper.*	+	–
2.	Yes, a newspaper is made of paper. Say that statement.	*A newspaper is made of paper.*	+	–
3.	What material is a board made of?	*Wood.*	+	–
4.	Say the statement about a board.	*A board is made of wood.*	+	–
5.	What material is a window made of?	*Glass.*	+	–
6.	Say the statement about a window.	*A window is made of glass.*	+	–
Pass = 5/6 or more correct (Not pass = more than 1 error)			P	NP

D. Opposites

•	You're going to make up statements that have the opposite word.			
1.	The children do math after recess. Say a statement that tells the opposite about when the children do math.	*The children do math before recess.*	+	–
2.	Ricky will throw the football. Say a statement that tells the opposite about what Ricky will do.	*Ricky will catch the football.*	+	–
3.	He painted the fence after he painted the garage. Say a statement that tells the opposite about when he painted the garage.	*He painted the fence before he painted the garage.*	+	–
4.	We couldn't wait for the movie to start. Say a statement that tells the opposite about what we couldn't wait for.	*We couldn't wait for the movie to end.*	+	–
Pass = 4/4 correct (Not pass = 1 or more errors)			P	NP

E. Map Reading
Material: Map, page 15 (or Workbook, Lesson 65, Side 2)

1.	Touch **A.** Which direction is that arrow pointing?	*West.*	+	–
2.	Touch **B.** Which direction is that arrow pointing?	*South.*	+	–
3.	Touch **C.** Which direction is that arrow pointing?	*East.*	+	–
4.	Touch **D.** Which direction is that arrow pointing?	*North.*	+	–
Pass = 4/4 correct (Not pass = 1 or more errors)			P	NP

14   *Language Assessment Handbook*

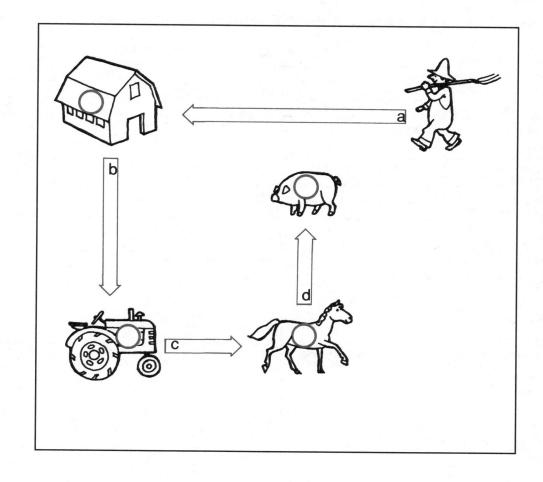

Individual Score Sheet—Assessment 8

Student Name _____ Date _____

(Present each item. Circle + or – for each response. Responses must be verbatim unless enclosed in parentheses.)

A. Synonyms

			+	–
1.	Tell me a synonym for **thin**.	Skinny.	+	–
2.	Tell me a synonym for **closed**.	Shut.	+	–
3.	Tell me a synonym for **big**.	Large.	+	–
4.	Tell me a synonym for **small**.	Little.	+	–
			P	NP

Pass = 4/4 correct (Not pass = 1 or more errors)

B. True—False

			+	–
•	I'm going to make up statements. Some of these statements are true and some are false. You tell me about each statement.			
1.	Chickens give milk. True or false?	False.	+	–
2.	You cannot eat metal. True or false?	True.	+	–
3.	Shoes can be made of leather. True or false?	True.	+	–
4.	Monkeys do not have wings. True or false?	True.	+	–
5.	Make up a statement about shoes that is true.	(Accept reasonable answer.)	+	–
6.	Make up a statement about shoes that is false.	(Accept reasonable answer.)	+	–
			P	NP

Pass = 5/6 or more correct (Not pass = more than 1 error)

C. Who—What—When—Where—Why

			+	–
•	Listen to this story.			
•	The pilot was flying an airplane. She saw a big storm coming, so she landed the airplane at an airport. After the pilot landed, the passengers got out of the airplane.			
•	Listen again. (Repeat the story.)			
1.	Tell what the pilot was flying.	(An airplane.)	+	–
2.	Tell where the pilot landed the airplane.	At an airport.	+	–
3.	Tell who got out of the airplane.	The passengers.	+	–
4.	Tell why the pilot landed.	(She saw a big storm coming.)	+	–
5.	Tell when the passengers got out of the airplane.	(After the pilot landed.)	+	–
			P	NP

Pass = 4/5 or more correct (Not pass = more than 1 error)

D. Analogies

			+	–
•	You're going to make up analogies about a purse and a bottle and money and water. The analogy tells what you put in the container.			
1.	What do you put in a purse?	Money.	+	–
2.	What do you put in a bottle?	Water.	+	–
3.	A purse is to money as a bottle is to . . .	Water.	+	–
4.	Say the analogy that tells what you put in the containers.	A purse is to money as a bottle is to water.	+	–
			P	NP

Pass = 4/4 correct (Not pass = 1 or more errors)

E. Can Do

			+	–
1.	Can a man write on an envelope?	Yes.	+	–
2.	Say the statement.	A man can write on an envelope.	+	–
3.	Can a man sleep in an envelope?	No.	+	–
4.	Say the statement.	A man cannot sleep in an envelope.	+	–
5.	Make up another statement that tells something a man can do with an envelope.	(Accept reasonable answer.)	+	–
6.	Now make up a statement that tells something a man cannot do with an envelope.	(Accept reasonable answer.)	+	–
			P	NP

Pass = 5/6 or more correct (Not pass = more than 1 error)

Group Writing Part A—Assessment 9

Materials for Part A: Make a copy of Writing Assessment 9, Part A (page 18), for each student.

Note: Assessment 9 has two sections. The first section (Part A, which appears below) is a sentence-writing test that can be administered in a group setting or can be administered individually. The second section (Parts B–F) appears on page 19 along with the score sheet section for Part A.

1. (Hand out Writing Assessment 9, Part A, to the students.)
- (Teacher reference:)

Student Name _____ Date _____

| car   toad   bug |

_____

_____

_____

_____

- Write your name at the top of the page. √
2. You're going to write sentences that rhyme.
3. Touch the picture of the car and the bug. √
- The picture shows the car on something and the bug on something. What is the car on? (Signal.) *A road.*
- What is the bug on? *A toad.*
4. Say the sentence for the car. Get ready. (Signal.) *The car is on a road.*
- Say the sentence for the bug. Get ready. (Signal.) *The bug is on a toad.*
5. (Repeat step 4 until firm.)
6. The word box shows how to spell the words **car, toad,** and **bug.** You can figure out how to spell the other words.
7. Write the sentence for the car. Remember to start with a capital and end with a period. Pencils down when you're finished. (Observe students, but do not give feedback.)
- Now go to the next line and write the sentence for the bug. Pencils down when you're finished. (Observe students, but do not give feedback.)
8. (Collect student papers.)
9. (Score writing assessments using Part A criteria at the top of the Individual Score Sheet.)

car   toad   bug

_____

_____

_____

_____

Student Name _____ Date _____

(Present each item. Circle + or – for each response. Responses must be verbatim unless enclosed in parentheses.)

A. Sentence Writing

1.		(Both sentences begin with a capital and end with a period.)	+	–
2.		(Sentence 1:) *The car is on a road.*	+	–
3.		(Sentence 2:) *The bug is on a toad.*	+	–
4.		(All word box words are spelled correctly: **car, toad, bug.**)	+	–
5.		(Legible writing.)	+	–
Pass = 4/5 or more correct (Not pass = more than 1 error)			P	NP

B. Calendar Facts

1.	How many weeks in a year?	52.	+	–
2.	How many days in a year?	365.	+	–
3.	How many seasons in a year?	4.	+	–
4.	How many months in a year?	12.	+	–
Pass = 4/4 correct (Not pass = 1 or more errors)			P	NP

C. Analogies

•	You're going to figure out what an analogy is about. Listen. A restaurant is to eating as a hotel is to sleeping.			
1.	What class are a restaurant and a hotel in?	*Buildings.*	+	–
2.	A restaurant is to eating as a hotel is to sleeping. Does our analogy tell what the buildings are made of?	*No.*	+	–
3.	Does our analogy tell what you do in the building?	*Yes.*	+	–
4.	Our analogy tells what you do in them. What do you do in a restaurant?	*Eat.*	+	–
5.	Say the first part of the analogy.	*A restaurant is to eating.*	+	–
6.	What do you do in a hotel?	*Sleep.*	+	–
7.	Say the next part of the analogy.	*A hotel is to sleeping.*	+	–
8.	Say the whole analogy.	*A restaurant is to eating as a hotel is to sleeping.*	+	–
Pass = 7/8 or more correct (Not pass = more than 1 error)			P	NP

D. Who—What—When—Where—Why

•	Listen to this story.			
•	The cow was in the pasture. It was noontime. The sun was bright, so she closed her eyes. A fly came up to the cow and sat on her back. The cow scared the fly away by swishing her tail.			
•	(Repeat the story.)			
1.	Tell what the cow did to scare away the fly.	(Swished her tail.)	+	–
2.	Tell where the cow was.	(In the pasture.)	+	–
3.	Tell who sat on the cow's back.	(A fly.)	+	–
4.	Tell why the cow closed her eyes.	(The sun was bright.)	+	–
5.	Tell when the cow closed her eyes.	(Noontime.)	+	–
Pass = 4/5 or more correct (Not pass = more than 1 error)			P	NP

E. Map Reading

•	Stand up.			
1.	Face west. (If child does not respond correctly in 3 seconds, point west, and say, "This is west." Circle minus and repeat item 1.)	(Child faces west.)	+	–
2.	What are you doing?	*Facing west.*	+	–
3.	Face north.	(Child faces north.)	+	–
4.	What are you doing?	*Facing north.*	+	–
5.	Face south.	(Child faces south.)	+	–
6.	What are you doing?	*Facing south.*	+	–
7.	Face east.	(Child faces east.)	+	–
8.	What are you doing?	*Facing east.*	+	–
Pass = 7/8 or more correct (Not pass = more than 1 error)			P	NP

F. Synonyms

•	I'm going to make up a story. You're going to say the story, too, but you are going to use synonyms.			
1.	There was a boy who was very thin. Say that statement.	*There was a boy who was very thin.*	+	–
2.	Say that statement with a synonym for **thin.**	*There was a boy who was very skinny.*	+	–
3.	This boy really liked to shout. Say that statement.	*This boy really liked to shout.*	+	–
4.	Say that statement with a synonym for **shout.**	*This boy really liked to yell.*	+	–
5.	One day he got in the closet and closed the door. Say that.	*One day he got in the closet and closed the door.*	+	–
6.	Say that statement with a synonym for **closed.**	*One day he got in the closet and shut the door.*	+	–
Pass = 5/6 or more correct (Not pass = more than 1 error)			P	NP

Language Assessment Handbook   **19**

Group Writing Part A—Assessment 10

1. (Hand out Writing Assessment 10, Part A, to the students.)
- (Teacher reference:)

Student Name _____ Date _____

short   boat   sail

_____
_____
_____
_____

- Write your name at the top of the page. √
2. You're going to write sentences that rhyme.
3. Touch the picture of the cat and the boat. √
- The picture shows what kind of tail the cat had and what kind of sail the boat had. The cat had a short tail. The boat had a big sail.
- What kind of tail did the cat have? (Signal.) *A short tail.*
- What kind of sail did the boat have? (Signal.) *A big sail.*
4. Say the sentence for the cat. Get ready. (Signal.) *The cat had a short tail.*
- Say the sentence for the boat. Get ready. (Signal.) *The boat had a big sail.*
5. (Repeat step 4 until firm.)
6. The word box shows how to spell the words **short, boat,** and **sail.** You can figure out how to spell the other words.
7. Write the sentence for the cat. Remember to start with a capital and end with a period. Pencils down when you're finished. √ (Observe students, but do not give feedback.)
- Now go to the next line and write the sentence for the boat. Pencils down when you're finished. √ (Observe students, but do not give feedback.)
8. (Collect student papers.)
9. (Score writing assessments using Part A criteria at the top of the Individual Score Sheet.)

short   boat   sail

_____

_____

_____

_____

Individual Score Sheet—Assessment 10

Student Name _____ Date _____

(Present each item. Circle + or – for each response. Responses must be verbatim unless enclosed in parentheses.)

A. Sentence Writing

1.		(Both sentences begin with a capital and end with a period.)	+	–
2.		(Sentence 1:) *The cat had a short tail.*	+	–
3.		(Sentence 2:) *The boat had a big sail.*	+	–
4.		(All word box words are spelled correctly: ***short, boat, sail.***)	+	–
5.		(Legible writing.)	+	–

Pass = 4/5 or more correct   (Not pass = more than 1 error) | | | P | NP

B. Analogies

•	You're going to make up an analogy that tells what you do on a table and a chair.			
1.	Tell me what class a table and a chair are in.	*Furniture.*	+	–
2.	Tell me what you do on a table.	(Accept reasonable response.)	+	–
•	Let's say you eat on a table.			
3.	Tell me what you do on a chair.	(Idea: Sit on it.)	+	–
•	Yes, you sit on a chair.			
4.	Say the analogy about what you do on a table and on a chair.	*A table is to eating as a chair is to sitting.*	+	–
5.	What does our analogy tell about each piece of furniture?	(What you do on it.)	+	–

Pass = 4/5 or more correct   (Not pass = more than 1 error) | | | P | NP

C. Who—What—When—Where—Why

•	Listen to this story.			
•	The girl was in school. She told a funny joke. The children laughed because they liked the joke. After the children stopped laughing, they all went back to work.			
•	(Repeat the story.)			
1.	Tell what the girl did.	(Told a funny joke.)	+	–
2.	Tell why the class laughed.	(They liked the joke.)	+	–
3.	Tell who went back to work.	(The children; all of them.)	+	–
4.	Tell when the children went back to work.	(After they stopped laughing.)	+	–
5.	Tell where the girl was.	(In school.)	+	–

Pass = 4/5 or more correct   (Not pass = more than 1 error) | | | P | NP

D. Synonyms/Opposites

•	Tell me if I name synonyms or opposites. Think big.			
1.	**Easy. Difficult.** Are they synonyms or opposites?	*Opposites.*	+	–
2.	**Shout. Yell.** Are they synonyms or opposites?	*Synonyms.*	+	–
3.	**Thin. Skinny.** Are they synonyms or opposites?	*Synonyms.*	+	–
4.	**Healthy. Sick.** Are they synonyms or opposites?	*Opposites.*	+	–

Pass = 4/4 correct   (Not pass = 1 or more errors) | | | P | NP

E. Statements

1.	Listen to this statement. Yesterday Cheryl played baseball. Say that statement.	*Yesterday Cheryl played baseball.*	+	–
2.	Does that statement tell what Cheryl is doing now?	*No.*	+	–
3.	Does that statement tell who Cheryl played with?	*No.*	+	–
4.	Does that statement tell what Cheryl did yesterday?	*Yes.*	+	–
5.	Does that statement tell you if Cheryl wore a coat?	*No.*	+	–
6.	Name two things that statement does not tell you.	(Accept reasonable responses.)	+	–

Pass = 5/6 or more correct   (Not pass = more than 1 error) | | | P | NP

F. Description

•	I'm going to say two things about something you know. See if you can figure out what I'm talking about.			
•	(Hold up one finger.) **Dorns** is the name of a big class. (Hold up two fingers.) Dorns have roofs and walls.			
1.	Tell me what you know about dorns. (Hold up one finger.)	*Dorns is the name of a big class.*	+	–
2.	(Hold up two fingers.)	*Dorns have roofs and walls.*	+	–
3.	Tell me what dorns are.	*Buildings.*	+	–
•	Here's another one. (Hold up one finger.) Nerp is an action. (Hold up two fingers.) When you nerp, you chew food and swallow it.			
4.	Tell me what you know about nerp. (Hold up one finger.)	*Nerp is an action.*	+	–
5.	(Hold up two fingers.)	*When you nerp, you chew food and swallow it.*	+	–
6.	Tell me what nerping is.	*Eating.*	+	–

Pass = 5/6 or more correct   (Not pass = more than 1 error) | | | P | NP

1. (Hand out Writing Assessment 11, Part A, to the students.)
   - (Teacher reference:)

Student Name _____ Date _____

| cow   walk |

_____
_____
_____
_____

- Write your name at the top of the page. √
2. You're going to write sentences that do **not** rhyme.
3. Touch the picture of the cow and the cat. √
   - The picture shows what the cow will do and what the cat will do. The cow will walk. The cat will sit. What will the cow do? (Signal.) *Walk.* Yes, walk.
   What will the cat do? (Signal.) *Sit.*
4. Say the sentence for what the cow will do. Get ready. (Signal.) *The cow will walk.*
   - Say the sentence for what the cat will do. Get ready. (Signal.) *The cat will sit.*
5. (Repeat step 4 until firm.)
6. The word box shows how to spell the words **cow** and **walk.** You can figure out how to spell the other words.
7. Write the sentence for what the cow will do. Remember to start with a capital and end with a period. Pencils down when you're finished. √
   (Observe students, but do not give feedback.)
   - Now go to the next line and write the sentence for what the cat will do. Pencils down when you're finished. √
   (Observe students, but do not give feedback.)
8. (Collect student papers.)
9. (Score writing assessments using Part A criteria at the top of the Individual Score Sheet.)

cow   walk

_____

_____

_____

_____

Individual Score Sheet—Assessment 11

Student Name _____ Date _____

(Present each item. Circle + or – for each response. Responses must be verbatim unless enclosed in parentheses.)

A. Sentence Writing

1.		(Both sentences begin with a capital and end with a period.)	+	–
2.		(Sentence 1:) *The cow will walk.*	+	–
3.		(Sentence 2:) *The cat will sit.*	+	–
4.		(Both word box words are spelled correctly: **cow, walk**.)	+	–
5.		(Legible writing.)	+	–

Pass = 4/5 or more correct   (Not pass = more than 1 error)   P   NP

B. Opposites

•	The ham is cooked. Say the statement.	*The ham is cooked.*		
1.	Say a statement that tells the opposite about the ham.	*The ham is raw.*	+	–
•	The bed was narrow. Say the statement.	*The bed was narrow.*		
2.	Now say a statement that tells the opposite about the bed.	*The bed was wide.*	+	–
•	The park was near. Say the statement.	*The park was near.*		
3.	Now say a statement that tells the opposite about the park.	*The park was far.*	+	–

Pass = 3/3 correct   (Not pass = 1 or more errors)   P   NP

C. Synonyms/Opposites

•	Tell me if I name synonyms or opposites. Think big.			
1.	**Crying. Weeping.** Are they synonyms or opposites?	*Synonyms.*	+	–
2.	**Deep. Shallow.** Are they synonyms or opposites?	*Opposites.*	+	–
3.	**Small. Little.** Are they synonyms or opposites?	*Synonyms.*	+	–
4.	**Quickly. Slowly.** Are they synonyms or opposites?	*Opposites.*	+	–

Pass = 4/4 correct   (Not pass = 1 or more errors)   P   NP

D. Analogies

•	I'm going to say some analogies about a cat and a lion.			
1.	See if you can figure out what each analogy **tells** about the animals. Listen to this analogy. A cat is to small as a lion is to . . .	*(Big.)*	+	–
2.	Say that analogy.	*A cat is to small as a lion is to (big.)*	+	–
3.	What does that analogy tell about the cat and the lion?	(Idea: *What size the animals are.*)	+	–
4.	Listen to the next analogy. A cat is to meowing as a lion is to . . .	*Roaring.*	+	–
5.	Say that analogy.	*A cat is to meowing as a lion is to roaring.*	+	–
6.	What does that analogy tell about the cat and the lion?	(Idea: *What each animal says.*)	+	–

Pass = 5/6 or more correct   (Not pass = more than 1 error)   P   NP

E. Classification

•	We can put an oak tree into four different classes. The biggest class is living things. You'll name four classes, starting with the smallest class.			
1.	What's the smallest class for an oak tree?	*Oak tree(s).*	+	–
2.	What's the next bigger class?	*(Trees.)*	+	–
3.	What's the next bigger class?	*(Plants.)*	+	–
4.	What's the biggest class?	*(Living things.)*	+	–
5.	What is one kind of object you would find in all those classes?	*An oak tree.*	+	–
6.	Would you find a palm tree in all those classes?	*No.*	+	–
7.	Name three of those classes you would find a palm tree in.	*(Trees, plants, living things.)*	+	–

Pass = 6/7 or more correct   (Not pass = more than 1 error)   P   NP

F. Verb Tense

•	It's time for some statements.			
1.	The boy will jump. What does that tell you?	(Idea: *What the boy will do.*)	+	–
2.	The boy jumped. What does that statement tell?	*What the boy did.*	+	–
3.	The boy is sitting. What does that statement tell?	*What the boy is doing.*	+	–
4.	The dog ran home. What does that statement tell?	*What the dog did.*	+	–
5.	The dog is sleeping. What does that statement tell?	*What the dog is doing.*	+	–

Pass = 4/5 or more correct   (Not pass = more than 1 error)   P   NP

   Language Assessment Handbook   **25**

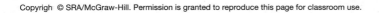

Materials for Part A: Make a copy of Writing Assessment 12, Part A (page 27), for each student.

Note: Assessment 12 has two sections. The first section (Part A, which appears below) is a sentence-writing test that can be administered in a group setting or can be administered individually. The second section (Parts B–F) appears on page 28 along with the score sheet section for Part A.

1. (Hand out Writing Assessment 12, Part A, to the students.)
- (Teacher reference:)

Student Name _____ Date _____

| boy | cat | girl |

- Write your name at the top of the page. √
2. You're going to write sentences that rhyme.
3. Touch the picture of the girl and the boy. √
- The picture shows what the girl had and what the boy had. What was the thing the boy had? (Signal.) *A cat.*
- The thing the girl had rhymes with **cat.** What was the thing the girl had? (Signal.) *A hat.*
4. Say the sentence for what the girl had. Get ready. (Signal.) *The girl had a hat.*
- Say the sentence for what the boy had. Get ready. (Signal.) *The boy had a cat.*
5. (Repeat step 4 until firm.)
6. The word box shows how to spell the words **boy, cat,** and **girl.** You can figure out how to spell the other words.
7. Write the sentence for what the girl had. Remember to start with a capital and end with a period. Pencils down when you're finished. √ (Observe students, but do not give feedback.)
- Now go to the next line and write the sentence for what the boy had. Pencils down when you're finished. √ (Observe students, but do not give feedback.)
8. (Collect student papers.)
9. (Score writing assessments using Part A criteria at the top of the Individual Score Sheet.)

boy   cat   girl

_____

_____

_____

_____

Individual Score Sheet—Assessment 12

Student Name _____ Date _____

(Present each item. Circle + or – for each response. Responses must be verbatim unless enclosed in parentheses.)

A. Sentence Writing

			+	–
1.		(Both sentences begin with a capital and end with a period.)	+	–
2.		(Sentence 1:) *The girl had a hat.*	+	–
3.		(Sentence 2:) *The boy had a cat.*	+	–
4.		(The word box words are spelled correctly: **boy, cat, girl.**)	+	–
5.		(Legible writing.)	+	–

Pass = 4/5 or more correct   (Not pass = more than 1 error)   P | NP

B. Description

			+	–
•	I'm going to say two things about something you know. See if you can figure out what I'm talking about. (Hold up one finger.) A metting is a tool. (Hold up two fingers.) You can use a metting to cut meat.			
1.	Tell me what you know about a metting. (Hold up one finger.)	*A metting is a tool.*	+	–
2.	(Hold up two fingers.)	*You can use a metting to cut meat.*	+	–
3.	Tell me what a metting is.	*A knife.*	+	–
•	Here's another one. (Hold up one finger.) **Nerk** is a word. (Hold up two fingers.) **Nerk** is the opposite of **fast.**			
4.	Tell me what you know about nerk. (Hold up one finger.)	*Nerk is a word.*	+	–
5.	(Hold up two fingers.)	*Nerk is the opposite of fast.*	+	–
6.	Tell me what nerk is.	*Slow.*	+	–

Pass = 5/6 or more correct   (Not pass = more than 1 error)   P | NP

C. Statements

			+	–
1.	The girls are playing on the slide. Say that statement.	*The girls are playing on the slide.*	+	–
2.	Does that statement tell what the girls are doing now?	*Yes.*	+	–
3.	Does that statement tell what the boys are doing?	*No.*	+	–
4.	Name three things the statement does not tell us.	*(Accept reasonable responses.)*	+	–

Pass = 4/4 correct   (Not pass = 1 or more errors)   P | NP

D. Synonyms

			+	–
•	Let's make up statements that mean the same thing as other statements by using synonyms.			
•	The book is hard. Say that.	*The book is hard.*		
1.	Say the statement that means the same thing.	*The book is difficult.*	+	–
•	Here's another one. The ring is shiny. Say that.	*The ring is shiny.*		
2.	Say the statement that means the same thing.	*The ring is bright.*	+	–
3.	What's a synonym for **healthy?**	*Well (or good).*	+	–
4.	What's a synonym for **large?**	*Big.*	+	–
5.	What's a synonym for **under?**	*Below.*	+	–

Pass = 4/5 or more correct   (Not pass = more than 1 error)   P | NP

E. Verb Tense

			+	–
1.	The police officer waved. What does that statement tell?	*(What the police officer did.)*	+	–
2.	What did he do?	*Waved.*	+	–
3.	The turtle is swimming. What does that statement tell?	*What the turtle is doing.*	+	–
4.	What is it doing?	*Swimming.*	+	–
5.	The monkey will swing. What does that statement tell?	*What the monkey will do.*	+	–
6.	What will he do?	*Swing.*	+	–

Pass = 5/6 or more correct   (Not pass = more than 1 error)   P | NP

F. If—Then

			+	–
•	You're going to make up if–then statements.			
1.	Does a person get more work done when the person works hard or when the person doesn't work hard?	*When the person works hard.*	+	–
2.	Start with the words "If a person works hard," and say the whole statement.	*If a person works hard, the person gets more work done.*	+	–
3.	When will the vacuum cleaner work, when it is plugged in or when it is not plugged in?	*When it is plugged in.*	+	–
4.	Start with the words "If a vacuum cleaner is plugged in," and say the whole statement.	*If a vacuum cleaner is plugged in, it will work.*	+	–

Pass = 4/4 correct   (Not pass = 1 or more errors)   P | NP

Materials for Part A: Make a copy of Assessment 13, Part A (page 30), for each student.

Note: Assessment 13 has two sections. The first section (Part A, which appears below) is a sentence-writing test that can be administered in a group setting or can be administered individually. The second section (Parts B–F) appears on page 31 along with the score sheet section for Part A.

1. (Hand out Writing Assessment 13, Part A, to the students.)
- (Teacher reference:)

Student Name _____ Date _____

black   white

1. Write your name at the top of the page. √
2. You're going to write sentences about this picture.
3. Touch the picture of the toad and the bird. √
- The picture shows what will go in the white car and what will go in the black car. What will go in the white car? (Signal.) *A toad.*
- What will go in the black car? (Signal.) *A bird.*
4. Say the sentence that tells what will go in the white car. Get ready. (Signal.) *The toad will go in the white car.*
- Say the sentence that tells what will go in the black car. Get ready. (Signal.) *The bird will go in the black car.*
5. (Repeat step 4 until firm.)
6. The word box shows how to spell the words **black** and **white.** You can figure out how to spell the other words.
7. Write the sentence for the toad. Remember to start with a capital and end with a period. Pencils down when you're finished. √ (Observe students, but do not give feedback.)
- Now go to the next line and write the sentence for the bird. Pencils down when you're finished. √ (Observe students, but do not give feedback.)
8. (Collect student papers.)
9. (Score writing assessments using Part A criteria at the top of the Individual Score Sheet.)

black   white

_____

_____

_____

_____

Individual Score Sheet—Assessment 13

Student Name _____ Date _____

(Present each item. Circle + or – for each response. Responses must be verbatim unless enclosed in parentheses.)

A. Sentence Writing

			+	–
1.		(Both sentences begin with a capital and end with a period.)	+	–
2.		(Sentence 1:) *The toad will go in the white car.*	+	–
3.		(Sentence 2:) *The bird will go in the black car.* •	+	–
4.		(Both word box words are spelled correctly: **black, white.**)	+	–
5.		(Legible writing.)	+	–

Pass = 4/5 or more correct   (Not pass = more than 1 error)   **P** | **NP**

B. Verb Tense

			+	–
•	Let's play a statement game.			
1.	The teacher will talk. What does that statement tell?	*(Idea: What the teacher will do.)*	+	–
2.	Say the statement that tells what the teacher will do.	*The teacher will talk.*	+	–
3.	Now make up a statement that tells what the teacher did.	*The teacher talked.*	+	–
4.	Now make up a statement that tells what the teacher is doing.	*The teacher is talking.*	+	–

Pass = 4/4 correct   (Not pass = 1 or more errors)   **P** | **NP**

C. Contractions

			+	–
•	It's time for some questions and statements with contractions.			
	Do snakes have wings?	*No.*		
1.	Say the statement with a contraction.	*Snakes don't have wings*	+	–
	Does a shark have feet?	*No.*		
2.	Say the statement with a contraction.	*A shark doesn't have feet.*	+	–
	(Point to a girl.) Is she washing her hair?	*No.*		
3.	Say the statement with a contraction for **is not.**	*She isn't washing her hair.*	+	–
	(Point to yourself.) Am I washing my hair?	*No.*		
4.	Say the statement with a contraction.	*You aren't washing your hair.*	+	–

Pass = 4/4 correct   (Not pass = 1 or more errors)   **P** | **NP**

D. Absurdity

			+	–
•	Listen to this statement and figure out what is absurd about it.			
1.	A boy was three years older than his mother. Say the statement.	*A boy was three years older than his mother.*	+	–
2.	What's absurd about that statement?	*(Idea: A boy can't be older than his mother.)*	+	–
•	Here's another absurd statement. Figure out what's absurd about this one.			
3.	The oldest person in my family is almost as old as my brother. Say the statement.	*The oldest person in my family is almost as old as my brother.*	+	–
4.	What's absurd about that statement?	*(Idea: The oldest person in my family can't be younger than my brother.)*	+	–

Pass = 4/4 correct   (Not pass = 1 or more errors)   **P** | **NP**

E. Opposites

			+	–
•	I'm going to tell you a story. You have to know your opposites to follow this story.			
1.	There was a horse. It was the opposite of clean. What do you know about that horse?	*(Idea: It was dirty.)*	+	–
2.	The dirty horse met a dog. The dog was the opposite of slow. What do you know about that dog?	*(It was fast.)*	+	–
3.	The fast dog started to chase the horse. It chased the horse to a stream that was the opposite of near. What do you know about that stream?	*(It was far.)*	+	–
4.	The dirty horse jumped over the stream, but the dog didn't. The stream was the opposite of narrow. What else do you know about that stream?	*(It was wide.)*	+	–

Pass = 3/4 or more correct   (Not pass = more than 1 error)   **P** | **NP**

F. Who—What—When—Where—Why

			+	–
• •	Listen to this story. The boy and his sister were in the park. He told a funny joke. His sister laughed because she liked the joke. After she stopped laughing, the boy and his sister climbed a tree. (Repeat the story.)			
1.	Tell who told a funny joke.	*(Ideas: A boy; the boy; a brother.)*	+	–
2.	Tell why his sister laughed.	*(She liked the joke.)*	+	–
3.	Tell who climbed a tree.	*(The boy and his sister.)*	+	–
4.	Tell when they climbed a tree.	*(After she stopped laughing.)*	+	–
5.	Tell where the boy and his sister were.	*(In the park.)*	+	–

Pass = 4/5 or more correct   (Not pass = more than 1 error)   **P** | **NP**

Language Assessment Handbook   **31**

Names	Calendar Facts	Where—When	Classification	Same—Different	Actions	Opposites	Sequence	True—False	Actions	Same—Different
	A	B	C	D	E	A	B	C	D	E
	Assessment 1					Assessment 2				
Pass Criteria	5 / 6	4 / 5	4 / 5	4 / 4	5 / 6	6 / 7	5 / 6	5 / 6	8 / 9	4 / 4
	Record **P** or **NP**									
1										
2										
3										
4										
5										
6										
7										
8										
9										
10										
11										
12										
13										
14										
15										
16										
17										
18										
19										
20										
21										
22										
23										
24										
25										
Number who passed **P** / Total number of students										
Circle **R** for Group Remedy needed (if more than ¼ did not pass)	R	R	R	R	R	R	R	R	R	R

Group Summary Sheet—Assessments 3–4

Names	Only	Calendar	Classification	Opposites	Who—Where—When—What	Who—How—Why	From—To	Questioning Skills	Calendar	Classification
	A	B	C	D	E	A	B	C	D	E
	Assessment 3					Assessment 4				
Pass Criteria	4 / 5	4 / 4	4 / 4	4 / 4	4 / 5	4 / 4	4 / 4	4 / 5	4 / 4	4 / 5
	Record **P** or **NP**									
1										
2										
3										
4										
5										
6										
7										
8										
9										
10										
11										
12										
13										
14										
15										
16										
17										
18										
19										
20										
21										
22										
23										
24										
25										
Number who passed **P** / Total number of students										
Circle **R** for Group Remedy needed (if more than ¼ did not pass)	R	R	R	R	R	R	R	R	R	R

Group Summary Sheet—Assessments 5–6

	Who—What— When—Where—Why	Classification	Verb Tense	From—To	Description	Classification	True—False	Description	Map Reading	Opposites
	A	B	C	D	E	A	B	C	D	E
	Assessment 5					Assessment 6				
Pass Criteria	4 / 5	4 / 5	3 / 3	4 / 4	6 / 7	5 / 6	5 / 6	7 / 8	4 / 4	3 / 3
Names	Record **P** or **NP**									
1										
2										
3										
4										
5										
6										
7										
8										
9										
10										
11										
12										
13										
14										
15										
16										
17										
18										
19										
20										
21										
22										
23										
24										
25										
Number who passed **P** / Total number of students										
Circle **R** for Group Remedy needed (if more than ¼ did not pass)	R	R	R	R	R	R	R	R	R	R

Group Summary Sheet—Assessments 7–8

Names	Classification A	Statements B	Analogies C	Opposites D	Map Reading E	Synonyms A	True—False B	Who—What—When—Where—Why C	Analogies D	Can Do E
			Assessment 7					Assessment 8		
Pass Criteria	5 / 6	5 / 6	5 / 6	4 / 4	4 / 4	4 / 4	5 / 6	4 / 5	4 / 4	5 / 6
Names					Record **P** or **NP**					
1										
2										
3										
4										
5										
6										
7										
8										
9										
10										
11										
12										
13										
14										
15										
16										
17										
18										
19										
20										
21										
22										
23										
24										
25										
Number who passed **P** / Total number of students										
Circle **R** for Group Remedy needed (if more than ¼ did not pass)	R	R	R	R	R	R	R	R	R	R

Group Summary Sheet—Assessments 9–10

Names	Sentence Writing A	Calendar Facts B	Analogies C	Who—What—When—Where—Why D	Map Reading E	Synonyms F	Sentence Writing A	Analogies B	Who—What—When—Where—Why C	Synonyms/Opposites D	Statement E	Description F
	A	B	C	D	E	F	A	B	C	D	E	F
	Assessment 9						Assessment 10					
Pass Criteria	4 / 5	4 / 4	7 / 8	4 / 5	7 / 8	5 / 6	4 / 5	4 / 5	4 / 5	4 / 4	5 / 6	5 / 6
	*Record **P** or **NP***											
1												
2												
3												
4												
5												
6												
7												
8												
9												
10												
11												
12												
13												
14												
15												
16												
17												
18												
19												
20												
21												
22												
23												
24												
25												
Number who passed **P** / Total number of students												
Circle **R** for Group Remedy needed (if more than ¼ did not pass)	R	R	R	R	R	R	R	R	R	R	R	R

Group Summary Sheet—Assessments 11–12

Names	Sentence Writing A	Opposites B	Synonyms/Opposites C	Analogies D	Classification E	Verb Tense F	Sentence Writing A	Description B	Statements C	Synonyms D	Verb Tense E	If—Then F
	\ Assessment 11						\ Assessment 12					
Pass Criteria	4 / 5	3 / 3	4 / 4	5 / 6	6 / 7	4 / 5	4 / 5	5 / 6	4 / 4	4 / 5	5 / 6	4 / 4
	\ Record **P** or **NP**											
1												
2												
3												
4												
5												
6												
7												
8												
9												
10												
11												
12												
13												
14												
15												
16												
17												
18												
19												
20												
21												
22												
23												
24												
25												
Number who passed **P** / Total number of students												
Circle **R** for Group Remedy needed (if more than ¼ did not pass)	R	R	R	R	R	R	R	R	R	R	R	R

Group Summary Sheet—Assessment 13

	Sentence Writing	Verb Tense	Contractions	Absurdity	Opposites	Who—What—When—Where—Why
	A	B	C	D	E	F
	Assessment 13					
Pass Criteria	4 / 5	4 / 4	4 / 4	4 / 4	3 / 4	4 / 5
Names	Record **P** or **NP**					
1						
2						
3						
4						
5						
6						
7						
8						
9						
10						
11						
12						
13						
14						
15						
16						
17						
18						
19						
20						
21						
22						
23						
24						
25						
Number who passed **P** / Total number of students						
Circle **R** for Group Remedy needed (if more than ¼ did not pass)	R	R	R	R	R	R